Food

JOY GREGORY

LIGHTBOX
openlightbox.com

LIGHTBOX

Go to
www.openlightbox.com
and enter this book's unique code.

ACCESS CODE

LBXR8697

Lightbox is an all-inclusive digital solution for the teaching and learning of curriculum topics in an original, groundbreaking way. Lightbox is based on National Curriculum Standards.

STANDARD FEATURES OF LIGHTBOX

AUDIO High-quality narration using text-to-speech system

ACTIVITIES Printable PDFs that can be emailed and graded

SLIDESHOWS Pictorial overviews of key concepts

VIDEOS Embedded high-definition video clips

WEBLINKS Curated links to external, child-safe resources

TRANSPARENCIES Step-by-step layering of maps, diagrams, charts, and timelines

INTERACTIVE MAPS Interactive maps and aerial satellite imagery

QUIZZES Ten multiple choice questions that are automatically graded and emailed for teacher assessment

KEY WORDS Matching key concepts to their definitions

CONTENTS

Food in the United States

The U.S. food industry grows, processes, packages, and delivers food and drinks to stores and restaurants all over the world. Some of the food, such as fruit and vegetables, is sold fresh. Most is sold to companies that turn farm-grown products into food ingredients.

30 cents of every dollar spent on food covers **manufacturing and distribution**.

Nestlé is the largest **food company** by sales in the world.

3.8 million Americans work in the fast-food restaurant industry.

The food industry is a chain of related activities. The sector includes everything from planting seeds to trucking **livestock**, catching fish, and shipping fresh and processed foods. The largest area of the food industry is food manufacturing. It pays more than $83 million in wages and benefits.

Native Americans first taught European settlers how to grow crops such as corn. Settlers soon added other **commodities**. By the early 1900s, scientific discoveries such as refrigeration began to change the food business. Over time, people were able to buy more factory-produced foods, such as canned soups and sauces.

The food industry contributes about $992 billion a year to the U.S. economy. That accounts for 21 million full- and part-time jobs. Only 1 percent of those jobs are on the farms that grow food.

Food Then and Now

Innovations in the food business have changed what the world eats. Until the mid-1900s, most people ate food grown close to home. Today, the United States **exports** and **imports** food and beverages to and from all over the world.

Planting Seeds

Farmers used to plant seeds by hand. Today, machines do the work faster and better. Plows use air to push seeds into the ground, so the soil does not have to be dug up. This prevents soil **degradation**.

THEN

NOW

Preserving Food

Until the mid-1900s, many Americans preserved home-grown food with a process called "canning." Most food **preservation** now takes place in factories, where it meets strict legal standards.

THEN

NOW

One branch of food industry research focuses on how growers can produce food more efficiently. The number of people living on Earth grew to 7.3 billion over the last 100 years. With that number still rising, farmers need help to find better ways to grow more food.

Food safety is another area of important research. Food is transported over huge distances. The industry works hard to make sure food is not **contaminated** as it moves from producer to **consumer**. The U.S. Food and Drug Administration (FDA) oversees food safety. It also sets rules about how food companies label ingredients and explain nutritional contents.

Moving Food Safely

Farmers used to sell their milk, meat, and other produce directly to local customers. Today, refrigerated shipping containers move large amounts of food long distances by truck, train, and ship.

THEN

NOW

Creating New Foods

Food companies once processed food simply by preserving fresh produce. Today's industry spends more than $5 billion a year to create foods with specific benefits, such as heart health or improved digestion.

THEN

NOW

Food Production in the United States

The food sector accounts for only a small percentage of U.S. domestic products. However, the sector feeds 320 million Americans. Every state grows fruits, vegetables, or grains, or raises animals for food. Across the country, 34,000 processing plants turn raw crops and other products into food and beverages.

1 Grapes and Raisins
Fresno, California

Most U.S. grapes are grown in California. They are used to make wine and raisins. The Fresno area has more than 20 raisin processors and raisin-packing facilities. It also has a number of wineries.

2 Potatoes and Fries
Fargo, North Dakota

Potatoes are the biggest vegetable crop in the United States. Most are used for frozen and **dehydrated** products. The largest single grower is R.D. Offutt Company in Fargo, North Dakota.

3 Dairy and Cheese
Plymouth, Wisconsin

Wisconsin has more dairy cattle for its size than any other state. Its cheese plants make more than 3 billion pounds (1.4 billion kilograms) of cheese a year. The Sartori Company, in Plymouth, Wisconsin, wins many awards for its cheese and butter.

4 Packaging
Philadelphia, Pennsylvania

One of the world's largest producers of steel and aluminum cans for the food industry is based in Philadelphia, Pennsylvania. With annual sales of more than $8 billion, Crown is the world's second-largest producer of cans used by the beverage sector.

Food Production and the U.S. Economy

Food service companies and manufacturers contribute about 66 percent of the **gross domestic product (GDP)** linked to the food sector. Only 1 percent of the trillion dollars the industry raises comes from farm production. Another 1 percent is generated by food and beverage store sales.

Today, many food stores prepare their own food on the premises. Customers appreciate being able to buy fresh food and see how it is made.

Food services include businesses involved with making, transporting, and selling goods. The sector employs nearly 12 million workers. Food manufacturers buy products from more than 2 million U.S. farms. The products are processed into foods and beverages sold at 680,000 **retail** stores and food-service outlets. Food manufacturers employ more than 1.5 million people.

3.2 million Americans **work** in retail stores selling food and beverages.

Nearly **one-third** of all **food processing** jobs are in meat and poultry plants.

On average, Americans spend nearly 13 percent of their household income on food. That makes food the third-highest household expense for U.S. families, behind the costs of housing and transportation. In 2016, the average U.S. household spent $4,049 a year on food eaten at home. The average cost of food eaten away from home, in restaurants, fast-food outlets, coffee bars, or other outlets, equalled $3,154.

Timeline of Food Industry Events

Over time, the United States moved from an **agrarian** to an **industrialized** society. Demand for store-bought food increased. Interest in laws to protect food safety also rose.

1790 | 1800 | 1840 | 1860 | 1880

1841. Anne Pickett starts the first home cheese factory in Wisconsin. She makes butter and cheese.

1790. About 95 percent of Americans live in rural areas. They grow their own food and trade with neighbors.

1860s. Gail Borden invents a process to preserve condensed milk. Later, Borden **pioneers** the introduction of other preserved foods.

1939–1945. Consumer demand rises for canned meats, dehydrated potatoes, and powdered juice. These products were developed for soldiers in World War II.

Future. Food companies will develop new products to meet increased consumer demand for safe, affordable, and nutritious food.

1900 | **1950** | **1970** | **2000** | **THE FUTURE**

1906. The Pure Food and Drug Act requires factual labels to be displayed on food sold in the United States.

1980. The U.S. government publishes the first Dietary Guidelines for Americans. The guide helps people understand the link between food and preventable diseases and conditions, such as heart attacks.

U.S. Food in the World

The United States exports more fresh and processed food than any other country in the world. Every year, other countries buy more than $131 billion of food from the U.S. The biggest export customers for the U.S. food industry are China, Canada, and Mexico.

About 20 percent of the U.S. corn crop is exported. Most is exported as ingredients such as corn syrup, starch, and oil.

Animal exports include fish and seafood, animal fat, poultry meat and eggs, red meats, and dairy products. Plant-based exports are vegetables, vegetable oils, nuts, food grains, fruit, and beer. The top food exports are soybeans, meat and poultry, and corn.

More than half of the food exported from the United States has been processed into higher-value food products. Much of the increased demand for such higher-value foods comes from countries where increasing income levels mean people have extra money for food. Such countries include China and Mexico.

The United States is the world's **largest producer** of **fluid milk**.

More than **95 percent** of the spices **consumed** in the United States are imported.

Processed foods account for about $70 billion of total U.S. food exports. Export-market growth is especially strong for companies that produce high-value foods used to prepare meals. Food preparation products include pasta, cookies, processed vegetables, cheese, yogurt, honey, and jam.

In some food categories, the United States sells most of what it produces to other countries. It exports more than 70 percent of the tree nuts it grows. More than 50 percent of the rice and wheat grown in the United States is also sold as exports.

The United States also imports some food products. More than 95 percent of the coffee, cocoa, fish, and seafood consumed in the United States is imported. About one-third of the wine and sugar is imported. More than half of the fresh fruits and fruit juices are also imported. More than 40 percent of food imports are plant products.

The United States exports more than $6 billion in dairy, eggs, and honey every year. In 2014, these three foods topped the list of fastest-growing food exports.

Facing the Issues

The food industry makes a major contribution to the U.S. economy. The sector feeds people all over the world. It also provides millions of jobs. Those benefits aside, the sector operates amid challenges to some of its business practices.

In particular, food producers and processors face pressure to ensure their work does not harm the natural environment. Farmers are trying to reduce their use of artificial **fertilizers** that might harm the soil, for example. This also helps to keep chemicals from running off the land into rivers and streams. People concerned about animal welfare also monitor the food industry to ensure it improves how it cares for the livestock, fish, and seafood it harvests.

One important issue for the food industry is the welfare of animals. Farm animals, such as turkeys, are often raised in very cramped conditions.

Debate

Federal laws regulate how most food in the United States is processed, packaged, and labeled. Some people believe nutrition labels help consumers make healthier food choices. People can compare nutritional facts. Should labels be required to carry certain information?

YES

- Informed consumers are healthy consumers.
- Consumers want to make better choices about the foods they eat.
- Labels should make it easy to compare calories and nutrient data such as calories, protein, and salt and sugar content.

NO

- U.S. food companies already follow laws about food safety.
- Food safety laws already require companies to list product ingredients.
- It is not a company's job to teach consumers about nutrition.

Many consumers are rejecting the use of chemicals in intensive farming. They worry about the effects of chemicals on their health.

Looking to the Future

Science has changed the way food is produced, processed, and delivered. The amount of food produced by farms in the United States has more than doubled since 1948. Technologies related to refrigeration, heat processing, and dehydration have made it possible for more food to travel longer distances from producers to consumers. Moving forward, the industry will use its links with science to meet consumer demand for different food choices.

Information about the link between diet and health is increasing sales of foods that include more protein and fiber, and less sugar, salt, fat, and **trans fat**. Buyers also want more **organic** options. This means they can choose food that has been produced without the use of chemicals. These trends are developing alongside calls for more informative nutrition labels.

Food processors are also focusing on increased sales in the food-away-from-home (FAFH) category. This trend encourages the development of meal-delivery services. FAFH and food-at-home buyers also seek more convenience. This ranges from prewashed salad greens and precut meats for stir fries to prepackaged meals with healthier formulations. Consumers also want more nutritional information about the meals they have delivered.

There has been a rapid growth in the home delivery of fresh-food boxes. Such boxes sometimes include all the ingredients for specific recipes that customers can cook at home.

Careers in Food

About 11 percent of working Americans have jobs that are related to agriculture and the food industries that are not directly linked to farms. These jobs range from people who work at grocery stores to the millions of Americans employed by fast-food and fine-dining restaurants. Other employees work in processing plants or support the industry as scientists, accountants, or truck drivers.

Food Scientist
Food scientists make sure food is produced efficiently and safely. Some supervise product development and monitor quality. Others work in research or manufacturing. Some are employed by private companies, while others work for branches of government.

Duties: Work with others to ensure that healthy, safe, and appetizing food is delivered to consumers

Education: Bachelor's degree in food science or biochemistry

Interests: Chemistry, biology, and **toxicology**

Food Stylist
Food stylists make food look good. They work with chefs and marketers to create appetizing pictures of food for print, TV, and internet-based formats. Their work illustrates food packages, grocery store advertisements, magazine articles, recipes, and restaurant menus.

Duties: Arrange food to be photographed to capture the attention of consumers

Education: On-the-job experience and college or university training in photography and design

Interests: Design, photography, food, and food plating

Quality Assurance Manger
Quality assurance managers work in production and packaging departments of food businesses. They make sure processes meet requirements set by state and federal law. They help write company policies that assure food and worker safety, and teach others to follow them.

Duties: Oversee all aspects of a food product's manufacture

Education: Bachelor's degree in food science, management, or engineering

Interests: Chemistry, manufacturing, toxicology, and communications

Activity

Food Packaging Research Study

Most of the food consumers buy has been packaged by the food industry. Even fresh produce, such as fruits and vegetables, is often sold in plastic wraps or containers. Types of packaging affect fresh-food storage. Use this study to figure out what types of packaging are most useful for which products.

You will need these items:

- Notebook or paper
- Pen or pencil to record findings
- Colored pencils or paints

Instructions

1. Take your notebook and pen to your local grocery store and visit the fresh foods section. This is where the fruits and vegetables are stored. Record four different ways fresh foods are packaged.
2. Find examples of food, such as lettuce, apples, and oranges, that are sold both loose and in bags or hard-sided plastic containers. Does different packaging affect the price? Why might it be worth paying more money for packaged products?
3. Compare different kinds of packaging. Think about why the packages are different. Why are grapes and strawberries sold in different sizes of hard-body plastic shells? Why are potatoes, apples, and peppers sold in plastic bags with holes?
4. Write a hypothesis, or theory, about why you think produce is sold in different containers.
5. Test your hypothesis. Food scientists have discovered that different packaging is better for storing different foods. Take a potato, a green banana, and a grape. Put them all in one plastic bag and seal it tightly. Put the bag in a sunny window. Place another potato, green banana, and a grape in your refrigerator on a plate. Do not let the foods touch.
6. Wait 10 days. Note down what happened to the produce in each case. What did you learn from the experiment about packaging?

Quiz

Check out how much you have learned about food production in the United States. The answers to all these questions are in this book.

ONE
How much of their income do Americans spend on the food they eat?

TWO
What percentage of U.S. food imports are plant products?

THREE
What percentage of the U.S. workforce is employed by the food industry not linked to farms?

FOUR
What U.S. state has the most cattle for its area?

FIVE
When were the Dietary Guidelines for Americans first published?

SIX
How much of every dollar Americans spend on food goes on manufacturing and distribution?

SEVEN
What state grows more grapes than any other state in the United States?

EIGHT
What country produces the most fluid milk in the world?

NINE
Name one of the three countries that buys the most U.S. food exports.

TEN
How many Americans work in the food service industry?

ANSWERS

ONE Nearly 13 percent **TWO** More than 40 percent
THREE 11 percent **FOUR** Wisconsin **FIVE** 1980 **SIX** 30 cents
SEVEN California **EIGHT** United States
NINE China, Canada, or Mexico **TEN** 12 million

Key Words

agrarian: farm-based

commodities: agricultural products

consumer: a person who buys goods for personal use

contaminated: made impure, and so ruined

degradation: a process of injury or harm

dehydrated: dried out

exports: sells products to other countries

federal: related to central rather than state government

fertilizers: artificial chemicals that help crops grow

gross domestic product (GDP): the value of all goods and services produced in a given time and place

imports: buys goods from other countries

industrialized: factory-based

ingredients: foodstuffs used to make other foods

innovations: new ideas

livestock: animals raised for food, such as cattle, pigs, and poultry

organic: grown without using artificial chemicals

pioneers: is the first to do something

preservation: the preparation of food for storage through a process such as cooking, pickling, or canning

processes: in food, the act of turning several products into a new one

retail: sold in a store

trans fat: a fat linked to heart disease

toxicology: a branch of science that studies poisons

Index

LIGHTBOX

SUPPLEMENTARY RESOURCES

Click on the plus icon found in the bottom left corner of each spread to open additional teacher resources.

- Download and print the book's quizzes and activities
- Access curriculum correlations
- Explore additional web applications that enhance the Lightbox experience

LIGHTBOX DIGITAL TITLES

Packed full of integrated media

VIDEOS

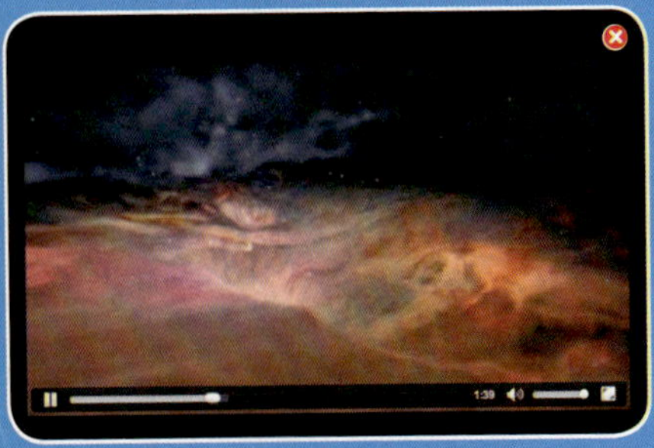

INTERACTIVE MAPS

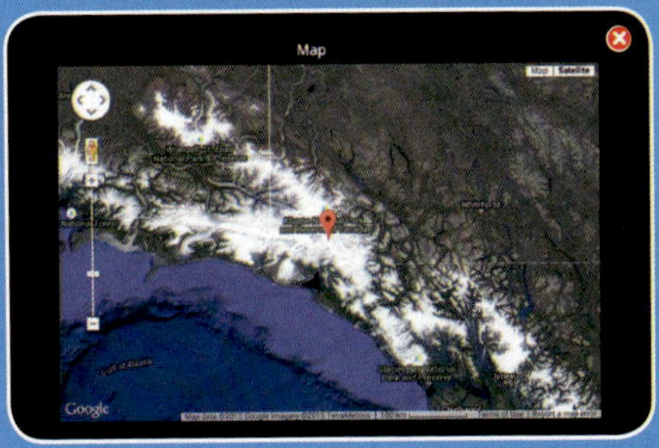

WEBLINKS

SLIDESHOWS

QUIZZES

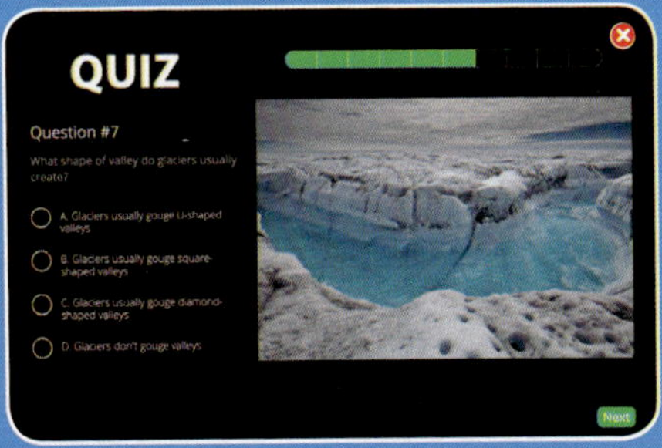

OPTIMIZED FOR

- ✓ TABLETS
- ✓ WHITEBOARDS
- ✓ COMPUTERS
- ✓ AND MUCH MORE!

Published by Smartbook Media Inc.
350 5th Avenue, 59th Floor New York, NY 10118
Website: www.openlightbox.com

Project Coordinator: Heather Kissock
Art Director: Terry Paulhus

Library of Congress Cataloging-in-Publication Data
Names: Gregory, Joy, author.
Title: Food / Joy Gregory.
Description: New York, NY : Smartbook Media Inc., [2018] | Series: American industries
Identifiers: LCCN 2017055659 (print) | LCCN 2017056496 (ebook) | ISBN 9781510535596 (Multi User ebook) | ISBN 9781510535589 (hardcover : alk. paper)
Subjects: LCSH: Food--United States--Juvenile literature.
Classification: LCC TX355 (ebook) | LCC TX355 .G792 2018 (print) | DDC 641.300973--dc23
LC record available at https://lccn.loc.gov/2017055659

Printed in Brainerd, Minnesota, United States
1 2 3 4 5 6 7 8 9 0 22 21 20 19 18

042018
120517

Every reasonable effort has been made to trace ownership and to obtain permission to reprint copyright material. The publisher would be pleased to have any errors or omissions brought to its attention so that they may be corrected in subsequent printings.
The publisher acknowledges Getty Images, Alamy, Newscom, Shutterstock, and iStock as its primary image suppliers for this title.